Beloved reader,
I'd like to express my deepest gratitude to the ones who have helped me write this story.

To the younger version of me who dared to dream.
To the future me who will flip through these pages,
cherishing every word.

To my ancestors, King David Dobbins & Sue Ella Dobbins-Walker, whose presence has been my North Star, guiding me through a cosmic journey.
To the family that raised me and nurtured me into the woman I am today.

To my lost loved ones whose names I will never forget:
Delton Heard, Christopher Kurdziel, Jeffrey Tyler Maddox, Andre Lamont McDonald, and John Hoogendoorn. May we meet again.

To the *hermanas por vida* who have been my keeper.

To every poet, writer, author, and artist that has inspired me along the way.

To future generations:
I pray that you find peace in the pain
and pleasure in the mundane,
for it is your voice
that will steer our fate.

Within you
is a world of pain
a world of pleasure
a world in which the two
blend together
to create
the universe inside of you

PAIN

Title	Page
Pain	6
Fathers	7
My Family Is an Ocean	10
Look to the Stars	12
The Fall	14
Rejection	15
I Survived	16
Ninth Hour	18
I Think I'm Tired of Love Poems	23
Ignite	24
Fight	28
Truth Lies	31
8:46	32
Grand Rapids	35
Independence Day	38
Miss Information	40

Pleasure

Title	Page
Pain & Pleasure	44
Miss Representation	45
I Made My Bed Today	48
This Version of Me	49
I Made My Bed Again	51
My Therapist Said	53
A Letter to the Better Version of Me	54
Crown	55
The Power of Now	56
Desire	58
Love	59
The Wind	62
Clay	63
Faith	65
Thought	66
Ten Things I Love About Me	67

PAIN

/pān/

NOUN
   physical suffering or discomfort caused by illness or injury.
   "she's in great pain"
   mental suffering or distress.
   "the pain of loss"
   an annoying or <u>tedious</u> person or thing.
   "she's a pain"
   careful effort; great care or trouble.
   "she took pains to see that everyone ate well"

VERB
   cause mental or physical pain to.
   "it pains me to say this"
   (of a part of the body) hurt.
   "sometimes my right hand would pain"

PAIN

Is more persistent than
Pleasure
Some may not see
it is the truth that
Pain will be here forever
And I cannot come to believe that
I can defeat this darkness
They say
It lingers forever
I don't know if it's true that
It comes then just as soon leaves
But it feels like
I could never turn this pain into
pleasure
I have always known that
Pain will forever be present
And I have no doubt that
Pain
Is more persistent than
Pleasure

Fathers

Fathers,
Be good to your daughters.
Because in America,
Black girls end up slaughtered
and we have to walk around
and act like we're unbothered,
but there's no heartbreak in the world
like one that comes from a father.

Fathers,
Be good to your daughters.
Because the love you give her now
might just make her smarter.
And she already lives in a world
where she has to work way harder,
and this distance you feel with her now,
well, it will only grow farther.

Fathers,
Please be good to your daughters.
'Cause they're killing girls like Breonna Taylor,
and we don't wanna be martyrs.
And the men won't protect us
'cause they say "that's not *my* daughter"
then coerce us
to givin' in
like our body's for barter

It's disheartenin'

Because I spent my whole life searchin'
and hopin'
that you would notice,
or just for a moment that you would focus.
You may not know this,
but sometimes, I really feel like I'm *soulless*
because this void is
so big that it could swallow me whole and,
that's why I wrote this
Because I've kept it all inside
for so long,
and I always wonder
if one day
you might just right these wrongs,
but I doubt it,
so I pour my whole heart into this song,
and all I wanted
was to truly feel like I belong.

So I say, fathers
be good to your daughters.
One day she'll be grown up
and heading off to college,
and some boy will try to convince her
not to be so modest,
and she'll question her very *worth*
because she lacked your guidance

You hear me, father?

I know you tried to be good to your daughter,
but I always felt like somethin' was missing,
did you really try your hardest?
I guess I turned out okay,
despite the bruisin'
and scarrin'
and the pain I buried deep inside
that they call *trauma*

and sometimes I really feel like
it was just me and my mama ...

and I still cry tears when I hear "No More Drama"
Like ...
*"No more drama in my life,
I don't ever wanna hurt again."*

But,
there's no heartbreak in the world
like one that comes from a father

So fathers,
just be good to your daughters.

My Family is an Ocean

My family is an ocean.
Vast, open
prayin'
hopin'
for smooth sails
But the waves keep crashin',
the storm seems to pass then,
something sweeps us off of our feet
onto the beach
of a foreign land ...

My family is the wind.
No beginning,
no end,
ever-moving, ever-reaching
spreading and seeping
into every edge of this planet

and maybe even beyond.

Beyond boundaries.
My family has never really been good at those,
but we reap what we sow because

My family is a tree.
Rooted so deep
that on the surface you can't see
just what that means to me.
To trace my leaves,

and the fruit that falls free
way back to the ancestors
who made it possible for me
by surviving seas,
and daring to dream,
connecting with constellations
so that I *might* be born free.

My family is the stars.
Even when we are worlds apart,
whether near or far,
their love lights my heart.
Because my family is vast
as a storm in the sea,
the breeze in the trees,
and everyone
and everything
in between
My family is all-inclusive,
because love knows no bounds.
Simple, yet profound.

My family is *LOVE.*

Look to the Stars

I don't know what it is that's got me feeling so ...
blue
Maybe
it's the rainy day and the clouds full of gloom.
Maybe
one of them damn planets is back on the move
or maybe
I need to make room.

Room to rest
because surely not every single moment in life is a test
that I fear I may fail
Created a cell in my mind, and I can't afford bail.
Looking for clues in my life but can't follow the trail.
It's like a boat in the ocean but no wind in my sail.

What is it that's got me feeling so ... stuck?
I want to keep moving but don't want to get up.
Don't always know my way forward
and sometimes want to give up
and steadily pouring myself over from an empty cup.

It's like ...
they always say that you reap what you sow,
but sometimes I see the reaper coming after my soul.
So much darkness all around and all the unknown,
but I need a little light if I ever will grow.

I know I'm not, but I still feel alone

I've lost loved ones along the way
I hope they've found a new home.
Somewhere where stars are the ones shooting,
not boys who think they're grown,
and they're waiting for me to make a trip of my own.
To the light,
where we fight for what's right,
and all those who came before are fighting side by side
to stop the evil in the world - all the greed and the pride
and we can wade in the waters of a beautiful life.

I hope I make it
to the other side
of this tunnel
but I still don't see the light.

I want to end it, but that just doesn't seem right.
So I keep going ...
and I still fight for my life like:

Chin up, head to the sky,
Keep fighting for your life.
It ain't easy, no, but believe me though ...
You won't know until you try ...

So when I look around,
and no light's to be found,
I look up to the stars
and know my ancestors are shining down.

The Fall

I never meant to fall
So hard so fast
I never meant to fall
Because I knew that love never lasts
I never meant to fall
And let you into my heart
I never meant to fall
Because I prefer to stay on guard
I never meant to fall
And I don't know if I can get up
I never meant to fall
But you just fill my cup
I never meant to fall
Into this world so full of bliss
I never meant to fall
But it seems that I got my wish
I never meant to fall
But they say it happens unexpected
I never meant to fall
But with you, I feel protected
I never meant to fall
But it feels so right within
I never meant to fall
But I'm so thankful that I did

Rejection

Not everything you seek is yours to keep
It may be sweet, at first
But bitterness leaves your taste buds sour.
Relinquish your power
over that which you cannot contain
Refrain from shifting blame,
lest you find yourself feeling
insane
and desperately grasping for anything to fill that gap.
Give it back.
Return the pain to its proper place.
It does not belong in your space.

Give it space

Give it time

Because in time,
all will be fine.
That which you seek,
you will find.
And when it's right, it will keep you.
You do not need it to complete you.
Just be you.

Rejection can liberate
Allow you to choose a different fate
where the pleasure of tomorrow
is not defined by the pain of today

I Survived

What is it like?

What's is like to be
the one so in controllably, in control of me?

How does it feel?
How's it feel to have the power to sink your teeth
so deep into me
getting right in between every dream I once dreamed
of making happy memories?

What were you thinking?
The first time you got that sweet taste of surrender?

Were you aware?
Did you know back then
that you were going to do it again and again
and again and again
and again and again
and AGAIN?

Numbing me from the inside out,
leaving me trying to figure out why the FUCK
this is what love
is supposed to be about?

Just one time ... did you ever feel bad?
Was there a single ounce in that sad sad soul
that begged and pleaded for you to just ...

Let me go?
Let me know!

What was it like?
That feeling of your fingers closing in around my neck?
Was it exciting? Arousing?
Did I deserve it? Did I earn it?
Because every plea I made,
you seemed to reverse it
Did you like it? Did you love it?
Because from where I'm lying, you sure don't look disgusted.

How many before me?
How many fucking girls before me
got stripped
of their humanity?
Humbled and humiliated?

How many after?
Oh, God
I can't even fathom

what is it like?

Ninth Hour

I've exhausted every avenue, every breath, praying for the inevitable to not be my reality.
You see, I have this tendency,
some call it a weakness,
to see people for the best.

I put so much faith
and love
into who a person could be,
that I ignore the bleak reality
of who they really are.
And it's not that I have a reason to.
I just do.
Time and time again people show me
and I still choose to believe that they are capable of being someone ... else.

Someone better.

I ignore the red flags,
those signs telling me to run away.
I sing along to songs that make me believe that
"if life was a movie then you ... "
you would be the best part.

I tell my intuition to pipe down because there's just got to be a reason.
I mean, everything happens for a reason, right?
And who am I to stop the Divine Plan?

Praying that we can overcome whatever demons have us in their grasp, I cling to those moments of bliss.
And I disregard those feelings of doubt.

I just want to believe that people are better than they are.

I have to.

I have to hang on by the silver thread of white lies ...
white lies that transform before my eyes
into seas of disappointment.
I knew it.
I had a feeling that this would fall apart.
But I stayed.
I wanted to.
Even after the storm, I thought ...
This is it. It cannot possibly get any worse than this.

I know pain too well.
I know abandonment too well.
I know how it feels to stay up late at night just wondering where exactly I went wrong.
Maybe if I just backtrack... just go back and go left instead of right then I wouldn't be feeling this way.
If only.
If only life was something that we could rewind.
We could reverse until we find
the one moment that turned our dreams into a catastrophe.
But this isn't Netflix.

We can't pause, rewind, and replay our favorite moments
just to avoid the ending that we overlooked.

The ending was inevitable.
Everyone told me it was.

And even as it was unfolding, I refused to believe that the
person who put me there was capable of causing that kind of
pain.

It makes me wonder ...
is there a part of you that takes pleasure in my suffering?
Did you ever wonder how long you could torture me with
words you never meant
and things you left unsaid
just so you could get some satisfaction?

Does it thrill you?
Does it make your heart flutter when you think about the
possibilities?
How long could this torture have endured?

The ending was inevitable.
You knew this.

But you still chose to put on a pretty face.
Paint a pretty picture and sell me a dream
that was never mine to hold onto.
I questioned God.

I know I'm not supposed to but
I questioned God.

In my own ninth hour, I questioned
my God, my God why hast thou forsaken me?

Why?
Why do I have to continuously endure
endless amounts of chaos?
I know they say
He gives his hardest battles to His strongest soldiers,
but I don't feel strong anymore.
I'm tired of fighting.
I'm tired of enduring.
I need to know that there's a purpose for the pain.

I desperately want to say that this will be the last time.
The last time I give so much, for so little.
The last time I put my blind faith into the hands of someone
so ready to destroy it.
As much as I desired for you to do better …
Be better
As much energy, love and passion as I give out …
I have to give to myself.
I can't keep winding down roads less traveled
and stopping along the way to smell every flower.
Because dandelions are just weeds in disguise.
But every seed of this weed carries a dream.
A wish for something better.

And when I close my eyes and
blow
I have faith.
I believe.
I choose to believe that this worthless weed will carry my wish somewhere beyond me.
Somewhere where a dream can become a reality.

It pains me to see the world around me so torn up.
So full of crushed hopes and lies that become the truth.
And truths that become lies.
I just have to believe that at any moment,
it just takes a decision.

One moment of realization that can change it all.

And maybe, just maybe
those moments of bliss would become obsolete
without the pain that I felt up until that point.

Maybe.

But I've exhausted every avenue,
every breath
longing for a reality that is not here.

I Think I'm Tired of Love Poems

I think I'm tired
of love poems
because when something goes wrong,
I wonder if the words will even make a difference
Or, if I'm just giving away
this precious
piece of me
to someone
who could easily
discard me.

While love poems
keep me locked in
to a dream
of a world that
has yet to begin
Yet,
I've given in.

Dreaming only of my lover
and forgetting about others
that want a piece of me,

especially me.

I think I'm tired
of love poems
that I can't write for me.

Ignite

What happens when the passion fades?
When the fire in your heart just
doesn't spark?
Do you force friction
to ignite a flame?
Do you just walk away?
Barricade
somewhere safe?
Somewhere warm
What's camping without fire
but a cold, dark night
As you look to the sky,
praying for light
and warmth
Shelter amid the storm
But instead
you see your breath
in the moonlight

What happens when the well runs dry?
Do you wait for the rain
to save the day?
Or make your way
to a lake
to quench your thirst?
But by the time you find
a body
of water to wade in,
it's rainin'

So you're back to seeking shelter
to weather
the next storm

And when the clouds finally roll away ...
and the sun finally peaks its face
are you grateful for another day?
Or, just anticipating the next disaster
like ...
What happens when your tent blows away,
just ...
whisked away by the wind?
When
your stash of rations is ravaged by raccoons, what do you do?

Is this what happens
when the passion fades?

Like ...
being lost in the wilderness
with nothing but your thoughts
and a prayer
that you dare
to believe
that
maybe a mustard seed
is all you need
But when the passion fades
it's hard to have faith,

hard to feel fire without a flame,
hard not to give up,
hard to drink from an empty cup
when weathering storm after storm with nowhere warm
to take refugee
Hard to sustain without food
and fathom what happens to you when the next storm comes
and there's nowhere to run

But ...
You look to the sun
and can't help but smile
because a while ago, you
prayed for its warmth
and when the well was dry, you
prayed for a storm
And when your tent was carried away by the wind,
some sailor on the lake prayed for it
And when your rations were ravaged by raccoons,
it was just a mother trying to feed her youth
and herein lies the truth

That you may not control what happens to you,
and you may not know what to do
when disaster takes root
but just as sure as the tides will change,
the sun will rise each day
and when the passion fades
we must find a way to fuel the fire in our heart

For there is no light
without dark

No dark without light

And the sun just might

Ignite

Fight

Fight like your life depends on it

Because it does.

Happiness is not granted to you just because
Sometimes it takes time ... and it really fucking hurts
But you have to fight, you have to heal
or it will only get worse.

Fight like your life depends on it

Because it does.

Because one day it might be better
than what it was
Don't expect it to be easy
because I promise you, it's not
But you gotta fight
and you gotta give it everything you've got

Mental health
is not something to fuck with
It's not bath bombs or hashtags
or something we hide in public
It's not something to be ashamed of
or something to cover
Because when we fail to recognize it,
we destroy one another

We all got patterns and bad decisions
that were passed down from momma
We're all so scared of something
and searching for peace from the drama
We all wish we had an account
with at least *one* damn comma,
but we let the pain swallow us whole
instead of resolving the trauma

This has got to end now
and it's got to be our generation
We can't keep letting curses from the ancestors
plague our nation
And sometimes the source of healing
just starts with conversation
And we gotta spread this love
the way we spread all this hatin'

Fight like your life depends on it
Because I promise, it does.

Happiness won't be given to us just because
And we won't find it while we mask our fears with food,
sex,
or drugs ...
but if you can't fight like your life depends on it,
will you fight like mine does?

Like your family, friends
and every life you've ever touched depends on it?

Because it does.

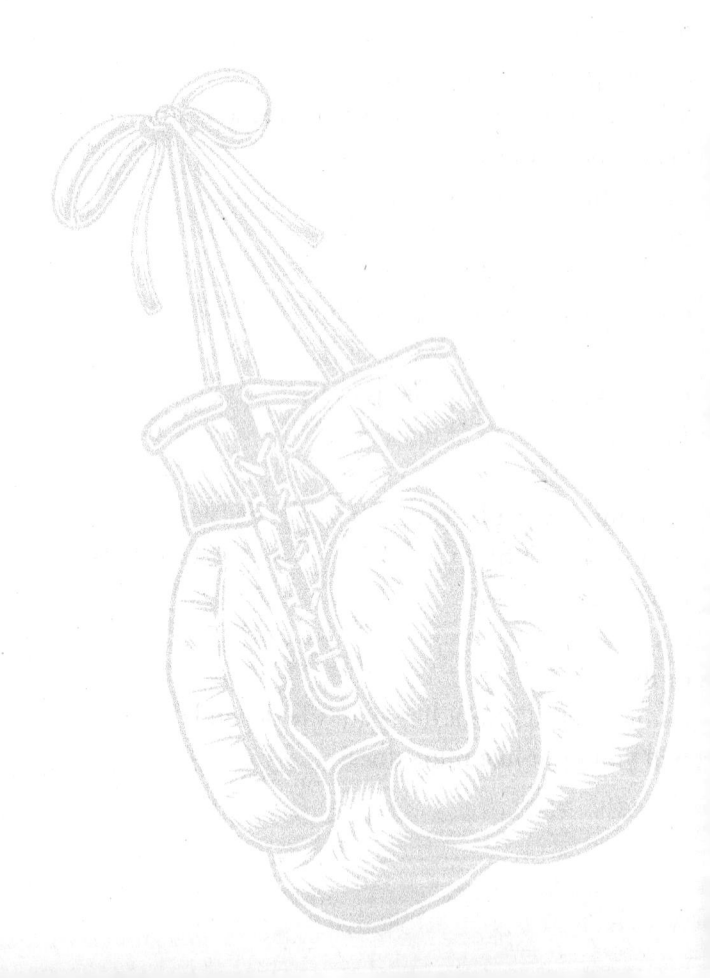

Truth Lies

Maybe truth lies
in the seams of our dreams
It seems that everything you see
Isn't really what it means
And if the truth lies ...
maybe so do we

Maybe
our beliefs
are limiting
our dreams
We cling
to our truth
and make it reality

Living in simulation, simultaneously

Collective truth lies in the systems we upkeep
Maintain so we can live in illusion
Destruction. Corruption. Greed. Pollution.
Things could be different,
but we're afraid of revolution
Because change is terrifying,
but we need evolution
Nothing lasts forever,
not even the lies
The truth could set us free
Or lead us all to demise

But truth lies

8:46

Wouldn't it be nice
if *all* lives mattered?
If we found a way to overcome the chatter?
If every human was truly treated with some decency
If there was really
liberation
from sea to sea?
You see,
it spreads way further than what you can see
but we know,
apples never fall too far from trees.

So today,
we are living with a legacy.
Slavery,
both physically and mentally,
and still, we are dealing with a strange fruit tree.
Its fruits,
yet another black or brown body
Then we tweet
the shit for the whole world to see.

And then we act surprised when the people start to riot.
When they're so fed up with generations of silence,
and the people walk around and act completely mindless
But your silence
is simply consent to violence.

See, Kanye said one day it *all falls down*
He told us *Jesus walks* before the levees went down

But nowadays we kind of wonder if this dude's a clown
' way he said slavery's a choice and wore the MAGA around
But shoot ...

I know we all just really want to improve
To see the children soak up knowledge
and go to a good school
We just want cops to please stop killing us
and caging us too
With those *subconscious* fears influencin' what they do

So what's up y'all?

What we gon' do with all this RAGE?
Do we destroy?
Destroy ourselves?
Our own community?
Or stay in this cage?
Do we riot?
Do we scream?
Do we wake up tomorrow and ...
It was all a *Dream*?

Do we chant *Black lives matter* in the streets
until our throats fucking bleed?!

What do we do?

When our lives are deemed *worthless?*

When we fail to look at every Black person
and see a purpose?
When no matter what we do or say ...
we're still getting killed
And now we're raising boys and girls
to live in fear that they've instilled

We're tired, exhausted
angry beyond words.
But ...
Welcome to *Amerikkka* -
how fucking absurd.

Sometimes I wonder
if we need to build a *free* Black nation,
Because I'm tired of repeating this damn conversation,
So ...

What if all lives mattered?
For *real*?
If just for a second
you'd imagine how it feels?
If everyone would stop pretending
and acting scared to address it?
So that we can overcome this,

or become another history lesson.

Grand Rapids

Stressed, yet at peace
Navigating giant waves, with ease
Despite what you believe, I'm the captain of this sea
Not a single ship has shit on me
Even the Titanic ... I move around, effortlessly,
with excellency,
I am the sea
The flow that connects every corner of each continent
Deeper than what you dare to dream,
the depths of me
are full of mystical creatures that eyes have never seen
I give grace to some
Some unworthy ships are still part of the *Grand Destiny*
Carrying jewels and treasure,
disease to strange places
Strange faces
Strange fruit
Fruit that bears truth
Fruit that takes root
wherever it lands
Whether stolen lands or the bottom of the ocean,
it's all a part of the *Master Plan*
Unfolding on a global stage
as spectators take their place within the Grand Stand.
Becoming a Grand Fan
of the Tom foolery,
distracted by the flashy jewelry
We forgot we are the jewel
we seek

We find
Because the waves keep a record of time
From Amistad to *Amerikkka*,
we've been here since the dawn
Moor power lies in the seed of our spawn
than we can contain
So make way
before we take way
Because these Rapids can get rough
And you're testing your luck
We're running out of fucks
to give
You're relying on grace,
but once we open the gates,
there's no going back
We're rallying behind everybody Black
Every body you attack with your lies and half-truths
The roof is on fire, and the well has run dry
The ceilings you've imposed can't contain what's inside
So let it burn

This light of mine ...
It comes from the Source
It is a force to be reckoned with, so act quick
because justice has set its course
through uncharted seas,
Rapid Rivers and Great Lakes
Think about what's at stake and take your place at the table
Grab a plate and eat at the fruits of your labors

Is the fruit bitter? Or sweet?
That which you've reaped?
Savor the Flavor that you created
and pray to your creator
that you've moved the needle far enough
to enter into the *Kingdom*
In the name of freedom
Of liberty
Of justice for all

We are one nation
Invisible
Indivisible
Inseparable from God
We respond
You've heard our cries and deceived us with lies,
but the people you refuse to see
are the *Universe's* eyes
Always watching. Always waiting. Always praying.
You may think you're preying
as you lie and exploit
Divide and destroy
Mirrors and smoke

We turn your smog into smoke signals and follow the code
The yellow, gold-paved, brick road
of a Promised Land
A land that is *Grand*
So, what is your *Master Plan?*

Independence Day

I find myself wondering why
N o matter how hard we try to pretend that we
D on't need
E ach other
P eople still decide to
E at alone
N eed to be alone in
D arkness ... We fear no
E vil, yet overlook the
N egativity we bring like
C hains wrapped around feet
E yes can see

Are we really free?

F or some
R eason, unknown
E vil still finds its way into
E very heart

Is there still a way to heal hearts and minds?

A separation of
P eople, places, things that
A rtificially create
R aces, with no reward
T hat spoils the
H umanity until
E ach
I ndividual is
D eprived

Are we better off apart?

T imes spent in
O ld kitchens with
G randparents that would give
E verything just
T o see a smile again, to
H old hands and hot pans
E very day until the day ends and then ... we
R ise to see another sunrise

Will we see another sunrise?

Miss Information

Who ... do you think you are?
Spreading lies like it's your North Star
Lies that sound like lullabies for silent nights with dark skies
that make you wonder ... *Why?*
Why have we embraced you?
Chased you
no matter how far from the truth you may be
Maybe ... we believe you
Maybe ... we need you
because
White lies pile up like Black lives and as a matter
of fact ...
we are too afraid to face you.
To see the truth in your eyes
that hides behind designer reading glasses ...
can you,
read between the lines?
Or, do you hide it all in the fine print?
So that we have to squint
just to make the truth evident?
It's evident that what was once deemed heaven-sent
seems to slither its way into psyches,
and phone screens,
and Apple TVs.
Even the trees are crying
as they see women and children dying,
while we watch blindly

What?!

What do we even do
when our votes feel more symbolic than sincere?
We're told to fear nothing but fear,
but is that not how we all got here?
How?
How are we to remain
free
and brave
when most of us don't even know what to say?
when most of us are too busy working our lives away
for a faulty system upheld by our fear of facing discomfort?
How did we get here?
How could we allow
all the lies and the hate to divide us like slices of a single pie?
Like the charts we see all over the news,
we confuse pie charts with truth,
and the truth is ...
They never wanted to make room for us at the table.
Where?
Where do we draw the line?
Or, can we gerrymander that too?
Then
fill it in with shades of blue
and red.
When will you meet your end, Miss Information?
Is there a glass ceiling somewhere just waiting for you to touch it?
To leave a single fingerprint just to prove that you *almost* broke through?

Or,
is the damage already done?
Have you, Miss Information
already won?

Pleasure

/ˈpleZHər/

NOUN
 a feeling of happy satisfaction and <u>enjoyment</u>.
 "she smiled with pleasure at being acknowledged"

ADJECTIVE
 used or intended for entertainment rather than business.
 "pleasure boats"

VERB
 give sexual enjoyment or satisfaction to.
 "tell me what will pleasure you"

Pain
Is more persistent than
Pleasure
Some may not see
It is the truth
Pain will be here forever
And I cannot come to believe that
I can defeat this darkness
They say
It lingers forever
I don't know if it's true that
It comes then just as soon leaves
But it feels like
I could never turn this pain into pleasure
I have always known that
Pain will forever be present
And I have no doubt that
Pain
Is more persistent than
Pleasure

Pleasure
Is more persistent than
Pain
And I have no doubt that
Pain will forever be present
I have always known that
I could never turn this pain into pleasure
But it feels like
It comes then just as soon leaves
I don't know if it's true that
It lingers forever
They say
I can defeat this darkness
And I cannot come to believe that
Pain will be here forever
It is the truth
Some may not see
Pleasure
Is more persistent than
Pain

Miss Representation

How you doing, Miss?
I see you, sis
Out here glowing and shining
bright like a diamond
in the rough.
Because this life you're livin', it must be tough.
Keepin' up with the trends,
surrounded by fake friends,
But ya nails done,
hair done,
everything *did!*

Miss
Representation,
How hard it must be
to survive in this nation,
where the women we see
don't look like you or me,
just bombshells and models
all over TV.

Between you and me,
something has got to change.
Black women are always the face,
but they won't show us the *range*.
They glorify our pain
make us feel insane ...
Oversexualize our bodies
to keep us locked in these chains.

And we can't speak the truth,
because it's viewed as a threat.
Too hostile or angry to earn their respect.
Mask emotions so we can be seen as perfect,
and every moment we stay silent fills our souls with regret.

Miss Representation,
Things change so much
from generation to generation
But when you peel back those layers,
not much has changed at all.
History's repeating,
and we need a wake-up call ...
Because we're sleepin'
through revolution,
and they want us all to feel small.
So, united we must stand,
or divided we shall fall.

So excuse me, Miss
I see you, sis!
Out here glowing and shining
bright like a diamond.

It takes pressure.
To become so great,
so beautiful and flawless,
despite your mistakes.
With the cards stacked against you,

you stare fear in the face.
And you're breaking glass ceilings of gender,
and race.

Miss Representation,
Don't you dare give up now!
Too many sacrifices have been made
to simply bow down.
Like a rose in concrete,
you emerge from the ground.
They try to box you in,
but you refuse to be bound.

I know heavy is the head that wears the crown.
Carrying burdens of injustice
that have been passed down.
But, together we are stronger,
and I know that now.
So keep representin'
and make the ancestors proud!

I Made My Bed Today

It's funny how
being around
your Southern, animated, 5-foot-two-inch,
hell-of-a-woman Granny
can make you see your world differently

She
speaks her mind
She
likes things to be a particular way
She
makes the pain fade away like sunlight on a rainy day
She
makes her bed every day

Granny,
I hope you love the woman I am becoming
as She
is a reflection of you.

We have much in common and
She
loves herself almost as much as
She
loves you and
She
makes her bed every day

This Version of Me

The version of me
when I was 23
is so close,
yet so far off
from the woman that I see.
It was 2018 when she almost lost her Dream
And at 23, that me you see
just wasn't as she seemed.
She,
shined real bright,
but fought the darkness inside.
She,
smiled all day,
then she cried every night.
She,
knew she had a purpose,
but her life was such a fight
to overcome the pain and
to find her inner light.
She trusted the wrong people,
and she loved the wrong men.
She made some dumb mistakes
then made the same mistakes again.

Because the version of me
when I was 23
is so close,
yet so far off
from the woman that I see.

THIS version of me
was not created easily.
Because for seasons all I'd see
was the loss and adversity.
But this version of me,
she fought all of that to be
exactly the me
that she was destined to be.
This version of me,
so,
at ease.
So unafraid to speak
'cause silence will not set you free.
This version of me,
so,
carefree.
Because she knows the me
that broke through
every shackle on her feet.

See, this version of me
simply would not be
without the version of me when I was 23
So if you're 23,
and you wanna learn a thing from me ...
Just don't lose faith,
and be exactly who you're meant to be.

I Made My Bed Again

I made my bed today.

And today I couldn't wait
to slip inside the covers,
close my eyes
And just ... Dream,
to imagine all the things I can be.

I'm better when my bed is made.

It sets the tone for the day because
when I come back home
to this sacred place,
I remember.
I surrender to me.
I believe.
I believe in the magic.
I believe that everything that's happened,
even moments that were tragic,
played their part.

It's art.

The creation of something new,
something inside of you ...
A dream that could be true, but
in order to dream,
you must close your eyes.
They say faith is like walking without sight

in the dark
with no sign of light ...
Until there is

Let there be light

I once was blind, but now
I see some things are beyond our control,
and the weight of it all takes its toll.
That's just how the story unfolds.
A fairy tale that will never grow old,
a story whose truth
is universal.
The story of growth
a story of hope
that the dark nights of the soul are followed by
a sunrise, and
as the sun peaks its way into my room
and I wake from a dream that almost felt real
a dream in which I had no fears
but the world that is real
is back here.
And eventually,
at the end of the day,
the light from the sun will still fade away
But, just for today ...
When I finally get home
I'm simply thankful
that I made my bed today.

My Therapist Said

My therapist said
I'm doing well
She can tell
That I've changed

But to me
In many ways
I have stayed
Exactly the same

A Letter to the Better Version of Me

With you, I feel complete
You see something in me worth fighting for
And I adore
the way you overcame the pain
that once consumed you
You took the shattered glass of the past
and put each piece in place, and
when I see your face in that mirror
It's clear that,
you
are all that I need
You
are my peace,
my calm in the storm
There's not a thing in this world I wouldn't do for you
It's true,
better version of me
I see you in my dreams, and I'd give anything to be
with you forever
Whether better or worse
Until death do us part
I will start with today ... and every day after
I will look you in the face and say
I love you
I love you, I love you, I love you,
I will place no one above you,
Dear, future version of me,

I hope you see what I see

Crown

I hope you wear it proud
That when they see it,
they bow down and worship you from the ground
all the way up to your crown
Adoring how it forms around your face,
adorned with grace,
and pain
and thorns that scrape
and flowers that bloom,
and family jewels passed down through generations,
now stationed upon your head
It's yours, this crown,
this throne
and you're finding a way
to make it your own
Yet,
you owe a great debt
to the ones who wore it first,
who had it worse,
whose birthright
was ripped from the womb

How do you bloom without roots?
Without truth?

Do you see it now?
Why you should be proud
of the power contained
within your crown?

The Power of Now

The mind is an interesting place
to *Be*
Because when you break free,
you see that nothing is ever quite what it seems.
It's filled with dreams,
but when you tap into the seams of those dreams,
you realize that the only dream is to *Be*.
To exist in a state of joy ...
to put suffering on hold
is to accept reality.
No resistance to what is.
No attachment to what was.
No fixation on what is yet to come.
Just here, now.

One day, when I'm rich all my problems will fade away ...
But that thought alone creates suffering today.
Then we waste the day
trying to make the pain fade away and are no closer
to the *Dream*.

The mind,
always running away from the past
or toward an uncertain future.
All that runnin' must be exhausting.
Must be easy to get lost in.
What's the cost?
Of living in the mind?
Being trapped inside the confines of time?

We project our fears
into our sphere of control.
They're pained in the stars of our soul ...
Sometimes a twinkle of hope
that's too far away to grasp.
So we create a mental map
that we think is the right path
to everything we need.
Everything we want to avoid.
Anything to fill this void.
But the void is all we need to truly see
that the essence of me lies beyond perceived reality

So just *Be*.

Be one with the life force of right *now*,
cast your burdens out,
and look around.

There is no greater power than the power of now.

Desire

It's desire that brings everything your heart sings about
to your doorstep.
Will you let it in?
Will you let yourself win ... for once?
For,
once upon a time, there was a time
when the subconscious mind was unaligned
and the heart sang with fear
Year, after year
The desire was clear:
to suffer.

Why would the heart want to suffer?

There's something safe about suffering,
something familiar about the pain,
so again, and again, this is what we choose
Though we have nothing to lose if we try something else
but our false sense of self.

Desire can inspire.
It can take you higher than you ever dreamed
It starts with a dream
It grows with belief
And you'll see
that thoughts mixed with feelings
Become things

So, who do you desire to be?

Love

Maybe love is the only way.

I've been contemplating this for a while now.
This ... purpose
for me
for my community
for humanity
I've been contemplating philosophies
and theories about what it all means,
and I think it all boils down to love.

For God so loved the world that he gave his seed
to teach
and die for us
To show us a glimpse of the raw vulnerability and love
the creator has for everyone
An experience of mortality that each of us faces,
and ultimately, a resurrection.
A plan for a new earth,
renewed and restored
to its divine nature and beauty.
But ... how do we get there?
Do we just spend our lives eating,
sleeping,
breathing
repeating ...
and waiting for the day that he makes all the pain fade away?

Can we even be saved?

Maybe it's up to us to cocreate the conditions by which we are all one,
each of us an expression of love.
For maybe if *we* so love the world,
we can save it.
Maybe while we sit and pray and wait for God,
he is waiting for us
to embrace his will and his plan
for each of us to be loved
and maybe we're just not ready yet.
Maybe we have some preparation to do.

Like, you know when you're about to have guests
and you clean the whole house from ceiling to floor?
And you make some food
then make some more
and what if that food
is the fruit of our labor?
Would it be bitter or sweet?
Just like a banana takes time to ripen,
we take time to evolve
to transcend and shift broken paradigms,
lies that tell us whose lives matter
and whose lives don't,
and we won't
find a Promised Land
until we keep our promise
to ourselves
and to one another.

and to everyone above, living amongst the stars,
some of them long forgotten,
too distant to see with the naked eye
but we must try
to change
together
because forever ...
is a long time
and what if forever could start now?

Maybe it already has.

Maybe we're all just projections from the past and a future
intertwined
with all life.

And maybe love is the only way that we see God's reflection
staring
at me
at you

Maybe it's true
that all you need is love.

The Wind

Sometimes
I can't help but notice how
everything around me seems to converge
How the people, places, potentials seem to emerge
from thin air
As if carried by the wind of my intentions
As if I'm destined to be here
Here, in awe
of the magic that surrounds us all
Just waiting to be recognized, to be noticed
to be held in this vessel
Harnessed and hoisted back into the air
to fill my sail
and carry my dreams overseas

Sometimes
I can't help but see
this invisible force inside of me
that steers my ship swiftly
and steadily making its way over miles of waves
to a place far beyond my sight
So I close my eyes and
just ride
Wind whistling in my ears whispering words only I can hear
Whisking away the fears of the day
as if nothing even matters but this moment
A moment that feels like forever

A moment that never ends
that moves like the wind

Clay

What do you do when your dream is so close
you can taste it
and you know if you choose to chase it,
it will be yours?
To have
To hold
To mold any way that you see fit
It fits so perfectly in your hand,
like clay that contours with every touch,
because everything you touch ...
Transforms
before your eyes to form gold where once was lead
Every thought that leaves your head
rearranges protons and electrons until
something new emerges from the soil of a fertile mind
The same soil that so generously nourishes
so life
can flourish and renew
The same soil whose clay fashioned you

You,
part clay
part stardust
You,
part matter, never created nor destroyed
part outside force that creates motion
part body of water filled with waves of emotion
You,
part mind whose thoughts travel faster than light

You,
part Source
part invisible force that holds it all together

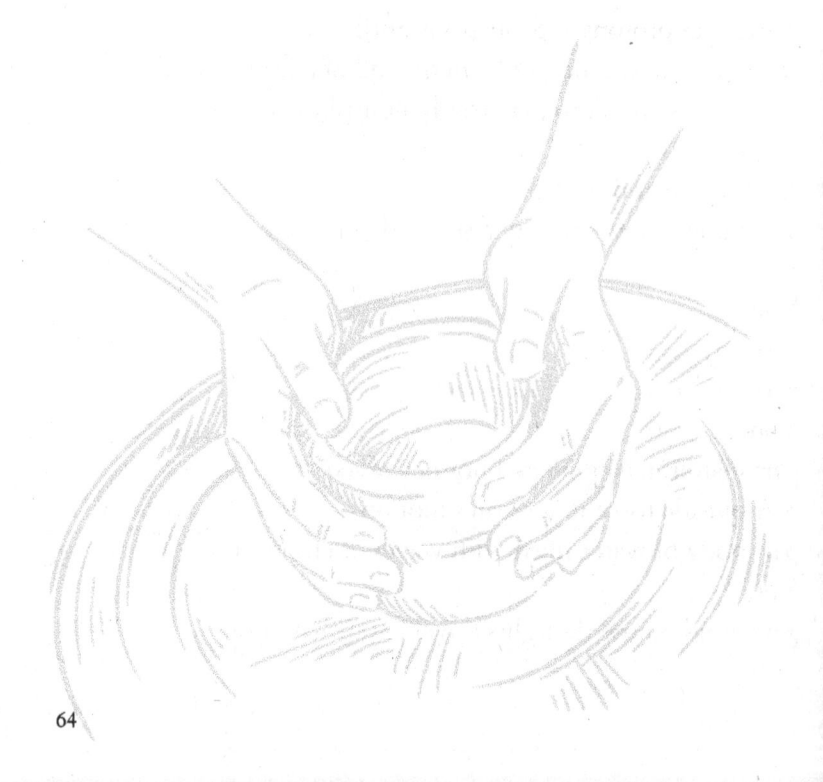

Faith

Fear has a funny way of fading away
When you choose to embrace

Faith.

Faith and fear can't live in the same space
and
When faith is in the building
It gets center stage

Just a mustard seed of

Faith.

And watch your worries fade away

Thought

The sound of silence fills the air with nothing but my
thoughts that drift away until they catch wind,
and then the next thought moves in
My thoughts used to be flooded with fear
with worry and doubt
Overflowing,
from knowing that without faith,
a thought becomes a violent wave.
These days my thoughts are full of dreams
of peace
Thoughts that, like a tree, branch out
reaching above until they kiss the sun
and when spring comes,
one by one, like leaves, they will grow
They will blossom into something new
because if seasons change,
so do you.

And it all begins
with a thought.

Sometimes in the quiet of the night
a seed is planted in my mind,
and it's hard to find the source
An unrecognizable, yet familiar, force
Like a voice
Like a guide inside reminding me that I'll be alright
That I don't even need sight because everything I need
is already inside.

Ten Things I Love About Me

TEN
I love the way that I use my pen
to paint pictures out of words
to reaffirm my worth
to search the depths of me and bring my dreams
into reality.

NINE
I love the way that I find
everything that was made for me
The way my mind is like a treasure map that
steers me through uncharted seas
until I find my way back
to the treasure buried deep inside of me.

EIGHT
I love the way that I strive to be great
The way I still make mistakes,
but when the stakes are high,
Still, I rise.

SEVEN
I love the way that the heavens align for me
with signs to see the rising star inside of me
that moves mountains with a mustard seed
This,
Divinity.

SIX
Yeah, I'm mixed
so I see the world quite differently
Because at another point in history,
my parents might be enemies
It's a mystery
how love conquers all
how it breaks every wall that was put in place
to separate by race,
but the antidote to hate
is love
and I am a product of
two star-crossed lovers who found one another
A White mother,
and a Black dad
Yeah, I'm mixed but what's sad
is that everyone seems to only see me as a fifty-percent
Half as if my being could be ripped apart
It breaks my heart, but the best part
is that I've learned how to be
one hundred and fifty-percent
Me.

FIVE
I love how I come alive
I have this
force inside the source provides
Ancestors guide, and
I love my life.

FOUR
I love how I hold the door open for others
even if they would slam one in my face,
I give grace
I find the strength to create a safe space
A place
where there are no doors.

THREE
I love each and every single version of me
from the worst of me to the woman I see now
I am humbled
yet proud
of how I've grown
from crawling to standing on my own

TWO
I love the way I transmute
the trauma and the pain
into something new
It's the way I believe
I can have, do, or be
anything I dare to dream
It's alchemy,
this magic inside of me could turn lead into gold
What I hold in my mind
I can hold in my hand
It's all a part of God's beautiful plan.

ONE
I love what I've done
I love how far I've come
to become a woman who shatters glass ceilings
Every fiber of my being burns
with a drive to change lives,
to heal hearts and minds
and I started with mine
Over time
I've seen each seed of intention grow
and I know that although
I love all the things I have done,
I have only just begun.

Beloved reader,

Thank you for exploring the universe that lives within me. I hope you have found a few parallels between our worlds and that you now see some of the threads that connect my universe to yours. This compilation has been years of heartbreaks, triumphs, questions, and realizations in the making, and it is a dream come true to place this piece of me into your hands. I have always believed that stories can change the world, but I never realized how much vulnerability came with the territory. Some of the closest people to me may read these pages and laugh. Some will cry. I imagine strangers flipping through these pages and somehow seeing themselves in my words. I imagine future generations reading these poems and becoming inspired to put their own pains and pleasures onto paper. I imagine myself holding the first printed copy and tearly shaking with the realization that I can't unwrite these words and I can't unlive the moments that filled these pages. But, I am so thankful that I continued to live and write this story, and I am thankful for the woman that I have become.

I pray that you, me, WE continue to tell our stories, no matter how painful they may be.

Our stories can set us free.

SHAYNA "AKANKE" MARIE IS A THOUGHT-PROVOKING WRITER, PASSIONATE POET, AND COMMUNITY ORGANIZER BASED IN GRAND RAPIDS, MICHIGAN WHOSE VOICE IS A RAW AND POWERFUL CALL FOR NARRATIVE JUSTICE AND COMMUNITY UNITY. RECOGNIZING THAT THOSE WHO POSSESS THE POWER TO DEFINE ALSO HAVE THE POWER TO DETERMINE, SHE HOLDS THAT DIVERSE NARRATIVES ARE PIVOTAL IN ENHANCING COMMUNITY OUTCOMES IN JUSTICE, EQUITY, AND INCLUSION. THROUGH POETRY, SHAYNA BRIDGES RACIAL AND GENERATIONAL DIFFERENCES, AND SHE HAS A PASSION FOR YOUTH ADVOCACY AND ENHANCING STUDENT OUTCOMES AND OPPORTUNITIES BY EMPOWERING STUDENTS TO SHARE THEIR STORIES WITH THE WORLD.

"When life knocks you down, roll over and look at the stars..."

WRITER. POET. ACTIVIST. CREATOR.